SUPER SANDCASTLE·
Let's Look A to Z

Arctic Ocean
to
Zimbabwe

Geography from A to Z

Mary Elizabeth Salzmann

Consulting Editor, Diane Craig, M.A./Reading Specialist

ABDO
Publishing Company

Published by ABDO Publishing Company, 8000 West 78th Street, Edina, Minnesota 55439. Copyright © 2009 by Abdo Consulting Group, Inc. International copyrights reserved in all countries. No part of this book may be reproduced in any form without written permission from the publisher. Super SandCastle™ is a trademark and logo of ABDO Publishing Company.

Printed in the United States.

Editor: Pam Price
Content Developer: Nancy Tuminelly
Cover and Interior Design and Production: Colleen Dolphin, Mighty Media
Photo Credits: Colleen Dolphin, iStockphoto/Terraxplorer, Peter Frischmuth/Peter Arnold Inc., Shutterstock

Library of Congress Cataloging-in-Publication Data

Salzmann, Mary Elizabeth, 1968-

  Arctic Ocean to Zimbabwe : geography from A to Z / Mary Elizabeth Salzmann.

    p. cm. -- (Let's look A to Z)

  ISBN 978-1-60453-013-1

  1. Geography--Juvenile literature. 2. English language--Alphabet--Juvenile literature. I. Title.

  G133.S28 2009

  910.3--dc22

                    2007050950

Super SandCastle™ books are created by a team of professional educators, reading specialists, and content developers around five essential components— phonemic awareness, phonics, vocabulary, text comprehension, and fluency— to assist young readers as they develop reading skills and strategies and increase their general knowledge. All books are written, reviewed, and leveled for guided reading, early reading intervention, and Accelerated Reader® programs for use in shared, guided, and independent reading and writing activities to support a balanced approach to literacy instruction.

About Super SandCastle™

Bigger Books for Emerging Readers
Grades K–4

Created for library, classroom, and at-home use, Super SandCastle™ books support and engage young readers as they develop and build literacy skills and will increase their general knowledge about the world around them. Super SandCastle™ books are part of SandCastle™, the leading preK–3 imprint for emerging and beginning readers. Super SandCastle™ features a larger trim size for more reading fun.

Let Us Know

Super SandCastle™ would like to hear your stories about reading this book. What was your favorite page? Was there something hard that you needed help with? Share the ups and downs of learning to read. We want to hear from you! Send us an e-mail.

sandcastle@abdopublishing.com

Contact us for a complete list of SandCastle™, Super SandCastle™, and other nonfiction and fiction titles from ABDO Publishing Company.

www.abdopublishing.com • 8000 West 78th Street Edina, MN 55439 • 800-800-1312 • 952-831-1632 fax

This fun and informative series employs illustrated definitions to introduce emerging readers to an alphabet of words in various topic areas. Each page combines words with corresponding images and descriptive sentences to encourage learning and knowledge retention. AlphagalorZ inspires young readers to find out more about the subjects that most interest them!

The "Guess what?" feature expands the reading and learning experience by offering additional information and fascinating facts about specific words or concepts. The "More Words" section provides additional related A to Z vocabulary words that develop and increase reading comprehension.

These books are appropriate for library, classroom, and home use.

Aa

Guess what?

Most of the Arctic Ocean has a thick layer of ice on it year-round.

Arctic Ocean

The Arctic Ocean covers the North Pole. An ocean is one of the huge saltwater bodies that cover most of the earth.

Arctic Ocean

Bay

A bay is part of a larger body of water such as a lake, sea, or ocean. It fills an area where the land along a coast curves inward.

Halawa Bay, Hawaii

Bayou

bayou

A bayou is a shallow stream that flows slowly. Bayous often form on flat land near large rivers.

Bb

Crater Lake

Crater Lake

Crater Lake is the deepest lake in the United States. The lake is in the crater of an extinct volcano. A crater is the hole in the middle of a volcano.

Cliff

Dover, England

A cliff is a high, steep surface of hard rock. Cliffs form when wind or water wears away the earth.

Cc

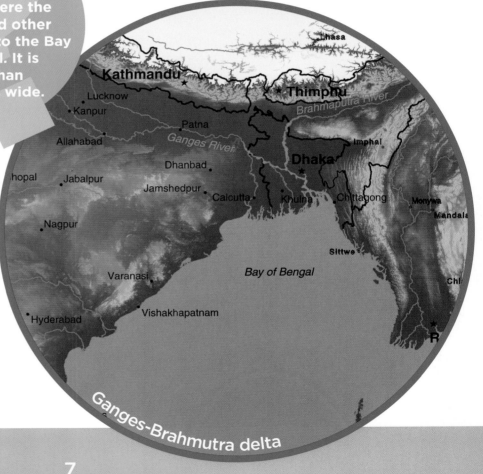

Delta

A delta is the area of land where a river flows into a lake, sea, or ocean. The river water spreads out into a triangular shape.

Ganges-Brahmutra delta

equator

Equator

The equator is an invisible line around the middle of the earth. It passes through 14 countries including Kenya, Colombia, and Brazil.

Ee

Everest

Mount Everest is the highest mountain in the world.
It is part of the Himalaya mountain range in Asia.
A mountain is an area of land that rises to a very high peak.

Mount Everest

Forest

A forest is an area that has a lot of trees growing close together. Forests are good places for many kinds of birds and animals to live.

Ef

forest

Guess what?

There are forests in all 50 states.

Old Faithful

Geyser

A geyser is a hot spring that shoots hot water and steam into the air. The water is heated by magma under the earth's surface.

Glacier

A glacier is a large body of ice that moves very slowly across the land. Glaciers never melt completely. The largest glacier covers most of Antarctica and is about a mile thick.

Glacier Bay, Alaska

Hawaii

Hawaii

The state of Hawaii is a group of islands in the Pacific Ocean. The largest island is also named Hawaii. An island is a piece of land surrounded by water.

Hemisphere

A hemisphere is half of a round object, such as a planet, moon, or star. The equator divides the earth into the Northern Hemisphere and the Southern Hemisphere.

Northern Hemisphere

Southern Hemisphere

Iceberg

iceberg

An iceberg is a large piece of ice that broke off of a glacier and fell into the ocean. Only a small part of an iceberg sticks up out of the water.

Guess what?

Some icebergs cover thousands of square miles.

Ii

Jenolan Caves

The Jenolan Caves are a series of limestone caves in Australia. They are over 300 million years old, which makes them the oldest known caves in the world. A cave is an underground chamber that can be entered through an opening on the surface.

Jj

Jenolan Caves

Kk

Kilimanjaro

Mount Kilimanjaro is a mountain created by a volcano. It has the highest mountain peak in Africa. A volcano is an opening in the earth's surface that lava shoots out of.

Mount Kilimanjaro

Guess what?

The highest peak of Mount Kilimanjaro is over 19,300 feet.

Lagoon

A lagoon is a shallow body of water along a coast. It is separated from an ocean or a sea by a reef, sandbank, or strip of land. There are also lagoons in the middle of atolls. An atoll is a ring-shaped coral reef.

lagoon

Madagascar

Madagascar is an island country in the Indian Ocean near Africa. It is the fifth-largest island in the world.

Mm

Mississippi River

The Mississippi River is the second-longest river in the United States. It flows from Minnesota to Louisiana. The Mississippi River was very important in the settling of the United States.

North Sea

The North Sea is part of the Atlantic Ocean. There are eight countries on the North Sea, including England and Germany. A sea is a section of an ocean. Some very large lakes are also called seas.

North Sea

Niagara Falls

Niagara Falls is a very wide waterfall on the border between Canada and the United States. There are two main parts, Horseshoe Falls and American Falls.

Niagara Falls

oasis

Oasis

An oasis is an area in a desert that has water, trees, and plants. The water usually comes from an underground spring. People traveling across a desert stop at oases to get water.

plain

Plain

A plain is a low, flat area of land that doesn't have trees. In the United States, the Great Plains cover parts of ten different states. South Dakota, Nebraska, and Kansas are three of the Great Plains states.

Peninsula

A peninsula is a large area of land that sticks out into an ocean. Alaska and Florida are both peninsulas.

Florida peninsula

Qq

Quicksand

Quicksand is an area of sandy ground mixed with a lot of water. If the water can't drain away, the sand gets so wet that objects sink into it. Usually the water that makes quicksand pushes up from underground.

quicksand

Guess what?

Quicksand does not suck things down into it. If you stay calm and move slowly, you can float in it.

Rio Grande

River

A river is a large stream of fresh water that flows into a lake or an ocean. Boats carry both people and goods on rivers.

Rain Forest

A rain forest is a wooded area that gets a lot of rain. Rain forests are usually in warm climates. The trees in rain forests are very tall, and their top branches spread out to form a layer called a canopy.

rain forest

swamp

Swamp

A swamp has areas of land mixed with areas of shallow water. Swamps are often located on the edges of rivers or lakes.

Ss

Sahara

The Sahara is a desert region in Africa. It is the largest hot desert in the world. A desert is an area of dry land that has few plants and gets very little rain.

Sahara

Timberline

Trees can't grow on some kinds of land or in some climates. A timberline is where land with trees meets land without trees. Tall mountains have timberlines because trees can't grow in very high altitudes.

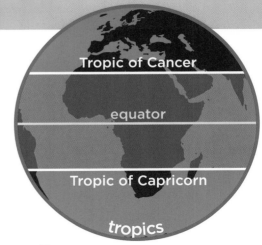

Tropics

The tropics are between the Tropic of Cancer and the Tropic of Capricorn. The tropics are the warmest places in the world.

San Juan Mountains

Uu

Underbrush

Underbrush is small bushes and plants that grow among trees. Birds and other animals use leaves and twigs from the underbrush to build nests.

undertow

Undertow

An undertow is a current beneath the surface of the water in an ocean or a large lake. An undertow is created when water flowing toward shore is pushed aside by water flowing back out to sea.

underbrush

Death Valley

Valley

A valley is a low area between hills or mountains. Many valleys have rivers running through them. A really deep valley may be called a canyon or a gorge.

Guess what?

Death Valley in California has the lowest spot in the United States.

Vv

Angel Falls

Waterfall

A waterfall is a stream of water that falls over the edge of a high surface, such as a cliff. The highest waterfall in the world is Angel Falls in Venezuela. Victoria Falls in Africa is the largest waterfall overall.

Ww

Xi'an, China

Xi'an is the capital city of Shaanxi province in China. The city was founded over 3,000 years ago. Today millions of people live in Xi'an.

Xi'an, China

Guess what?

Xi'an is pronounced she-AHN.

Yosemite National Park

Yosemite National Park is in California near the Sierra Nevada mountains. It was one of the first national parks created by the U.S. government. Yosemite is known for its granite cliffs and giant sequoia trees.

Yosemite National Park

Zambezi River

Zz

Zimbabwe

Zimbabwe is a country in Africa. The capital of Zimbabwe is Harare. The Zambezi River is on the border between Zimbabwe and Zambia.

Guess what?

Zimbabwe is a little bit bigger than Montana.

Glossary

altitude – the height of something.

canopy – a protective covering, such as an awning or high, leafy branches.

climate – the usual weather in a place.

divide – to separate into equal groups or parts.

drain – to draw off or remove a liquid bit by bit.

extinct – no longer active.

giant sequoia – an evergreen tree that has cones and can grow hundreds of feet tall.

goods – items that are bought and sold.

gorge – a deep, narrow passage between steep, rocky walls or mountains.

granite – a type of very hard rock made from cooled magma.

invisible – unable to be seen.

inward – toward the inside.

layer – one thickness of a material or a substance lying over or under another.

magma – melted rock below the earth's surface.

national – belonging to or taken care of by a nation's government.

opening – a hole that something can pass through.

overall – as a whole, with all things considered.

peak – the top of a mountain.

planet – one of the objects in space that go around the sun, such as Earth and Mars.

pronounce – to say correctly.

province – a geographical or governmental division of a country. Provinces are similar to states in the United States.

range – a row of things, such as mountains.

reef – a strip of coral, rock, or sand that is near the surface of the ocean.

sandbank – a large pile of sand.

shallow – not deep.

triangular – having a three-sided shape.

twig – a thin, small branch of a tree or a shrub.

underground – below the surface of the earth.

wooded – covered with trees.

More Geography!

Can you learn about these geography terms too?

Africa	fault	plateau
Antarctica	foothill	prime meridian
archipelago	glen	province
Asia	Great Salt Lake	ravine
Atlantic Ocean	gully	Red Sea
Australia	hill	ridge
Badlands	Hudson Bay	sea level
bluff	Indian Ocean	South America
canyon	marsh	Southern Ocean
Caribbean Sea	meadow	state
Catskill Mountains	Mediterranean Sea	steppe
cave	mesa	stream
channel	Mojave Desert	summit
continent	North America	territory
Dead Sea	ocean	time zone
desert	Pacific Ocean	tundra
elevation	panhandle	Uluru
Europe	Persian Gulf	water table